Robert Quackenbush's
TREASURY
OF HUMOR

DOUBLEDAY

NEW YORK · LONDON · TORONTO · SYDNEY · AUCKLAND

PUBLISHED BY DOUBLEDAY
a division of Bantam Doubleday Dell Publishing Group, Inc.
666 Fifth Avenue, New York, New York 10103

DOUBLEDAY
and the portrayal of an anchor with a dolphin
are trademarks of Doubleday,
a division of Bantam Doubleday Dell Publishing Group, Inc.

Library of Congress Cataloging-in-Publication Data applied for.

ISBN 0-385-26654-5

R.L. 2.8

Printed in Hong Kong

October 1990

First Edition in the United States of America

TEXT DESIGNED BY DIANE STEVENSON—SNAP•HAUS GRAPHICS

Program

Smart Alec Oration	6
JANUARY	7
Tongue Twisters	8
The Possum Pals and the Pickled Pepper Mystery	10
FEBRUARY	17
The Valentine Beaver	19
MARCH	25
Michael Finnegan	26
Limericks by Edward Lear	28
APRIL	31
There's a Flea in Lizzie's Ear	32
Detective Mole and the April Fools' Mystery	34
MAY	35
Jabberwocky by Lewis Carroll	36
My Mom Won't Allow	38
JUNE	39
Daddy's Whiskers	40
Henry the Duck Gets in Shape	42
JULY	47
Yankee Doodle	48
No Mouse for Me	50
AUGUST	55
Dr. Quack's Anatomy Lesson	55
Calling Dr. Quack	56
SEPTEMBER	59
Know Your Quacks	59
Know Your Duckalphabet	60
Detective Mole and the Chicken Coop Mystery	62
Back to School Jokes and Riddles	66
OCTOBER	67
There Was a Li'l Woman Who Took a Stroll	68
Monster Jokes and Riddles	70
NOVEMBER	71
Sheriff Sally Gopher and the Thanksgiving Caper	72
DECEMBER	83
The Nutcrackers and the Sugar Tongs by Edward Lear	84
The Boy Who Waited for Santa Claus	88
About the Captain of This Showboat	96

Smart Alec Oration

Ladles and jelly spoons:
I come before you
To stand behind you
And tell you something
I know nothing about.

Next Thursday,
Which is Good Friday,
There'll be a mother's meeting
For fathers only.

Wear your best clothes
If you haven't any,
And if you can come
Please stay at home.

Admission free;
Pay at the door.
Take a seat
And sit on the floor.

It makes no difference where you sit;
The man in the gallery is sure to spit.

The Possum Pals and the Pickled Pepper Mystery
~by R.Q.~

Patty Possum and his pal Percival finished their studies with the great Detective Mole. Then they set out to become detectives themselves. They nailed a sign on the tree where they usually hung out. The sign said:

DETECTIVE AGENCY

Then they waited and waited. But no cases came their way.

"I know," said Patty to Percival. "I'll go find a case somewhere. You stay here and take messages."

But Percival was not about to stay behind. So he followed Patty, but he kept out of sight.

Patty went walking down the road. It was snowing. He came to some little mounds along the road that were covered with the white snow. The snow made them look like white stepping-stones.

"Funny how the snow makes things look," he said out loud.

Joe Horse was standing nearby and heard him.

"Talking to yourself again, Patty?" he asked.

"I was just noticing how these little mounds along the road look like stepping-stones. By the way, have you heard the news? Percival and I have opened a detective agency. Could you use our services?"

"Not personally," said Joe Horse. "But here's a mystery for you:

> Peter Piper picked a peck
> Of pickled peppers,
> A peck of pickled peppers
> Peter Piper picked;
> If Peter Piper picked a peck
> Of pickled peppers,
> Where's the pickled peppers
> Peter Piper picked?"

"I don't get it," said Patty Possum.

"It's a case for you," said Joe Horse. "Find out what happened to Peter Piper's pickled peppers. He lost them and he has been trying to find them."

"Oh," said Patty. "You mean someone named Peter Piper could use the Possum Pals' Detective Agency to find his popled plickers—I mean pickled peppers?"

"Exactly," said Joe Horse. "Keep on the road until you come to the first house. That's where Peter Piper lives. Tell him Joe sent you."

"Thanks, I will," said Patty. And he went on his way. He came to Peter Piper's house and knocked on the door. The door opened and there stood Peter Piper.

"I'm a detective," said Patty. "Joe sent me."

"Please pass my portal," said Peter Piper.

Patty Possum went into the house and said, "Tell me everything you know about your missing pipled peepers—I mean pickled peppers," he said.

"Pleased as punch," said Peter Piper. "Proudly, I purchased a peck of pickled peppers."

"At the market?" asked Patty Possum, taking notes.

"Precisely."

"Go on," said Patty.

"My peck of pickled peppers were packed in a parcel and I promptly pedaled home," said Peter Piper.

"On a bicycle?" asked Patty.

"Precisely."

"Then what?" asked Patty.

"Precipitation prevented pedaling purposefully."

"You mean it began to snow, like today?"

"Precisely."

"And?" asked Patty.

"I pedaled to my portal and partook to pick my peck of pickled peppers from the parcel."

"They were gone!" said Patty.

"Precisely."

Patty Possum said, "There must be some clue as to what happened to those peopled pitchers—I mean pickled peppers. Do you still have the box they were packed in?"

Peter Piper went to another room and returned with an empty box. Patty Possum examined the box with his magnifying glass. He saw water stains and a broken corner at the bottom of the box.

"So that's it!" he said. "The mystery of your missing pipled plockers—oh, you know what I mean—is solved. Come with me and I'll show you where they are."

Together Peter Piper and Patty Possum left the house and went down the road to Joe's place.

"There are your you-know-whats," said Patty. "They are along the road underneath the snow. When I saw them I thought they looked like white stepping-stones. The jars fell out of the box when it became wet from the snow and ripped open. Then the jars fell along the road. Snow covered them and made them look like stepping-stones."

Patty closed his notebook.

"That will be five dollars for my services," he said to Peter Piper.

Just then Percival popped out of hiding and said, "Don't forget my share! We're partners, remember?"

So ended the Possum Pals' very first case.

The Valentine Beaver
~by R.A.~

It was the first day of February. Bert Beaver looked up from the new dam he was building. He saw Pete Rabbit hopping by with an armload of straw baskets.

"What's the hurry, Pete?" asked Bert.

"There's a basket sale in town," answered Pete. "I'm rushing these baskets home. Then I'm going back for more. I'm going to fill them with colored eggs. Easter is just a few months away, you know."

Pete Rabbit went on his way. When he was gone, Bert Beaver said aloud, "Straw baskets! Colored eggs! What a racket!"

Just then Bert's friends Chip Chipmunk and Vic Vole came by and heard him.

"What are you talking about, Bert?" asked Vic.

"I'm talking about Pete Rabbit's job," said Bert. "It's easy. Shopping for straw baskets to fill and hand out on Easter morning is not hard work. And for *that* Pete gets a big fuss made over him. He gets songs written about him and stories too."

Bert took a large bite of birch and the tree fell over.

"Now, *that's* work!" he said. "But does anyone care? No! I want to be the star of a holiday, just like Pete Rabbit is at Easter time."

"But all the holidays are spoken for," said Chip.

"That's what you think," said Bert. "What is the next holiday?"

"Soon it will be Valentine's Day," said Vic. "But it isn't really a holiday. Even so, it is an important day to a lot of folks."

"That's it!" said Bert. "Have either of you heard of the Valentine Beaver?"

"Why no," said Chip Chipmunk and Vic Vole together.

"Well, you have now," said Bert. "You're looking at him."

With that he stomped off and left Chip and Vic and the unfinished dam behind him. He went home and looked at his calendar. Valentine's Day was just two weeks away. It was on February 14, the same day he planned to finish his dam.

"The dam can wait," he thought.

Bert's plan was to make valentines and sign them with his new name: "The Valentine Beaver." Then he would slip them under doors early in the morning on Valentine's Day. When everyone woke up they would find valentines from the Valentine Beaver.

Pigs like mud,
Cows like squash!
I like you
I do, by gosh!

Roses are red,
Violets are blue,
What you need
Is a good shampoo,

"Everyone will be so happy," thought Bert. "I'll become as famous as Pete—the Easter Bunny! Grown-ups and children alike will be waiting for the Valentine Beaver to pay them a visit every year. Songs and stories will be written about me too."

He went shopping. He bought paper, paints, paste, and scissors. Then he began making valentines. It was harder than he thought it would be. He didn't know how to cut and paste and color very well. He only knew about building dams. Still, he kept on trying.

Days hurried by. Valentines and paper scraps nearly crowded Bert Beaver out of his house. But making them had not gotten any easier. Sometimes Bert would catch himself dreaming of dam building. But he would stop himself and work all the harder on his valentines.

One afternoon Chip Chipmunk and Vic Vole came knocking at Bert's door. Bert opened his door a crack and peeked out.

You be ice cream,
I'll be the freezer;
You be the lemon
And I'll be the squeezer.

Just as the vine
Grows round the stump,
You are my darling
Sugar lump.

Fiddle and bow,
Fish and sea,
Belong together,
Like you and me.

"Have you been sick, Bert?" asked Vic. "We've missed seeing you at the dam you were building."

"I've been busy," Bert replied.

"Busy at what?" asked Chip.

"You'll know in a few days," answered Bert. He closed the door.

Bert listened. When he was sure his friends were gone, he went to his closet. He looked at the costume he had just made to wear on Valentine's Day. He took it from the hanger. It was a white summer jacket that he had covered with red paper hearts.

Bert put on the jacket and stood in front of his mirror to see how he looked.

"What a surprise everyone has in store for them when they see the new me," he said. "I'm a star!"

Roses smell sweet,
So do you,
Nice perfume, dear;
Ah-ah-ah-CHOO!

At last Bert was ready. But on the day before Valentine's Day the weather became unusually warm for February. The snow began to melt. The creek, where Bert was building his dam, began to rise. Bert was worried that there would be a flood.

Suddenly being the Valentine Beaver didn't seem so important to Bert.

He ran to his dam to finish it fast and to stop the creek from flooding. All the animals in the community came to watch him work. Chip Chipmunk and Vic Vole were there and so was Pete Rabbit. When the dam was finished, everyone cheered.

Afterward Pete Rabbit said, "You're so lucky, Bert. I wish I could build dams. But I'm not good at building things."

If you think you are in love,
And still there is a question,
Don't worry much about it,
It may be indigestion.

Bert was surprised.

"But you can do things that I can't," he said. "You are a much better artist than I am, for one thing."

Then he thought of something.

"You've just given me an idea," Bert went on. "I can see that it would be a pretty dull world if we all did the same things. In fact, I know of a job that is more right for you than it is for me. Something besides your Easter Bunny job."

"What's that?" asked Pete.

"Come to my house tonight," said Bert, "and I'll tell you about it. But I'll give you a hint. Did you ever hear of the Valentine Rabbit?"

"Why no," said Pete.

"Well, you have now," said Bert. "I'm looking at him."

I like myself, I think I'm grand,
I go to the movies to hold my hand.
I put my arms around my waist,
And when I get fresh, I smack my face.

Michael Finnegan

moderately

There was a young man named Mi-chael Fin-ne-gan, He grew whis-kers on his chin-ne-gan, The wind came up and blew them in a-gain, Poor, poor Mi-chael Fin-ne-gan. Be-gin a-gain! There Fin-ne-gan. CUT!

2. There was a young man named Michael Finnegan,
   He went fishing with a pin again,
   Caught a fish and dropped it in again,
   Poor, poor Michael Finnegan. Begin again!

3. There was a young man named Michael Finnegan,
   He squawked up an awful din again,
   Because of that he could not sing again,
   Poor, poor Michael Finnegan. Begin again!

4. There was a young man named Michael Finnegan,
   He grew fat and then grew thin again,
   Then he croaked and had to begin again,
   Poor, poor Michael Finnegan. CUT!

Edited text by R.Q.

There was an Old Man with a beard,
Who said, "It is just as I feared!
 Two Owls and a Wren,
 Four Larks and a Hen,
Have all built their nests in my beard!"

There was an Old Man, on whose nose,
Most birds of the air could repose;
 But they all flew away
 At the closing of day,
Which relieved that Old Man and his nose.

There was a young lady of Firle,
Whose hair was addicted to curl;
 It curled up a tree,
 And all over the sea,
That expansive young Lady of Firle.

Limericks
by
Edward Lear

There was an old person of Dutton,
Whose head was as small as a button:
    So to make it look big,
    He purchased a wig,
And rapidly rushed about Dutton

There was a Young Lady whose bonnet,
Came untied when the birds sate upon it;
    But she said, "I don't care!
    All the birds in the air
Are welcome to sit on my bonnet!"

There was a young person of Ayr,
Whose head was remarkably square:
    On the top, in fine weather,
    She wore a gold feather,
Which dazzled the people of Ayr.

There was an Old man of Nepaul,
From his horse had a terrible fall;
 But, though split quite in two,
 With some very strong glue
They mended that man of Nepaul.

There was a Young Lady of Dorking,
Who bought a large bonnet for walking;
 But its color and size,
 So bedazzled her eyes,
That she very soon went back to Dorking

There was a Young Lady whose nose,
Was so long that it reached to her toes;
 So she hired an Old Lady,
 Whose conduct was steady,
To carry that wonderful nose.

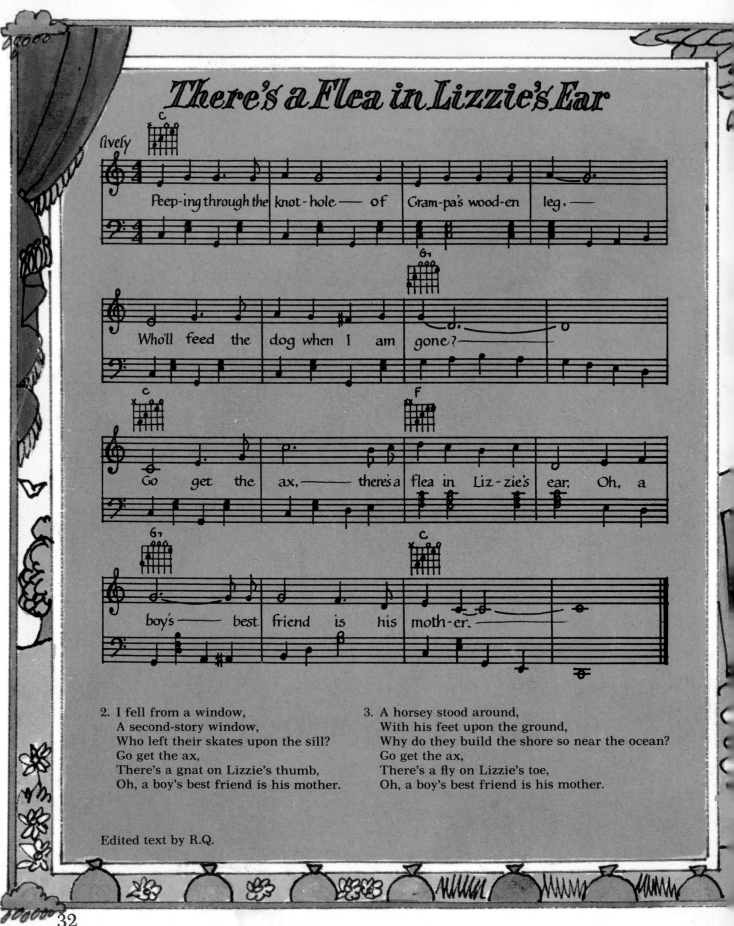

There's a Flea in Lizzie's Ear

lively

Peep-ing through the knot-hole — of Gram-pa's wood-en leg, —

Who'll feed the dog when I am gone? —

Go get the ax, — there's a flea in Liz-zie's ear, Oh, a

boy's — best friend is his moth-er. —

2. I fell from a window,
   A second-story window,
   Who left their skates upon the sill?
   Go get the ax,
   There's a gnat on Lizzie's thumb,
   Oh, a boy's best friend is his mother.

3. A horsey stood around,
   With his feet upon the ground,
   Why do they build the shore so near the ocean?
   Go get the ax,
   There's a fly on Lizzie's toe,
   Oh, a boy's best friend is his mother.

Edited text by R.Q.

Detective Mole and the April Fools' Mystery
~By R.Q.~

Max Squirrel came bursting into Detective Mole's office with a letter in his paw.

"Look what the postman delivered to me by mistake," he said. "This letter is for you. I think you won some money from a lottery."

Detective Mole took the envelope and looked at it. The front of the envelope was very plain. It had only his name and address scrawled on it. And there was no return address. But on the back of the envelope was a fancy gold seal. Sure enough, the envelope looked official—like it came from a lottery and that there might be money inside.

"Open it," said Max Squirrel. "You might have won a million dollars."

"Not likely," said Detective Mole. "APRIL FOOL!"

"Aw shucks," said Max. "I wanted to say that when you opened the envelope and saw nothing but fake money inside."

How did Detective Mole know that Max Squirrel was playing an April Fools' joke on him?

APRIL FOOL!

Detective Mole
Old Farm Road
City

ANSWER: Max had said that the postman had delivered the letter. There was no stamp on the envelope.

34

Jabberwocky

~ by LEWIS CARROLL ~

'Twas brillig, and the slithy toves
　Did gyre and gimble in the wabe;
All mimsy were the borogoves,
　And the mome raths outgrabe.

"Beware the Jabberwock, my son!
　The jaws that bite, the claws that catch!
Beware the Jubjub bird, and shun
　The frumious Bandersnatch!"

He took his vorpal sword in hand:
　Long time the manxome foe he sought.—
So rested he by the Tumtum tree,
　And stood awhile in thought.

And, as in uffish thought he stood,
　The Jabberwock, with eyes of flame,
Came whiffing through the tulgey wood,
　And burbled as it came!

One, two! One, two! And through and through
　The vorpal blade went snicker-snack!
He left it dead, and with its head
　He went galumphing back.

WHAT'S IN
THE MIDDLE
OF AN EGG
(THE LE

"And hast thou slain the Jabberwock?
    Come to my arms, my beamish boy!
O frabjous day! Callooh! Callay!"
    He chortled in his joy.

'Twas brillig, and the slithy toves
    Did gyre and gimble in the wabe:
All mimsy were the borogoves,
    And the mome raths outgrabe.

A DIRTY JOKE:
A WHITE HORSE
FELL IN THE MUD.

"G."

My Mom Won't Allow

Edited text by R.Q.

very quickly

My Mom won't al-low no pick-in' and a-sing-in' 'round here.

My Mom won't al-low no pick-in' and sing-in' 'round here. But

I don't care what my Mom won't al - low, do my pick-in' and a- sing-in'

an-y-how, My Mom won't al-low no pick-in' and a-sing-in' 'round here.

2. My Mom won't allow no guitar pickin' 'round here.
My Mom won't allow no guitar pickin' 'round here.
But I don't care what my Mom won't allow,
Gonna pick my guitar anyhow.
My Mom won't allow no guitar pickin' 'round here.

3. My Mom won't allow no banjo strummin' 'round here.
My Mom won't allow no banjo strummin' 'round here.
But I don't care what my Mom won't allow,
Gonna plunk my banjo anyhow.
My Mom won't allow no banjo strummin' 'round here.

Daddy's Whiskers

New text by R.Q.

lively

We have a dear ol' dad-dy, We love him ev'-ry day. He has a set of whis-kers, They're al-ways in his way.

Chorus:

Oh, they're al-ways in his way, Our horse eats them for hay, They grow in haste to dad-dy's waist, They're al-ways in his way.

2. Our daddy tried to shave them,
They grew right back that day.
He shaved them with a mower,
They grew back anyway.
        Chorus:

3. Our daddy went out chopping,
He struck a mighty blow.
It didn't stop his whiskers,
It helped to make them grow.
        Chorus:

4. Our daddy tried to blast them,
He bought some T.N.T.
The blasting didn't help him,
They grew right back, you see.
        Chorus:

41

Henry the Duck Gets in Shape

~by R.Q.~

The day Henry the Duck was taking his friend Clara to the movies, he weighed himself. Unknown to Henry, his bathroom scale was broken.

Henry was surprised to see that he had gained a lot of weight. He was worried that Clara might notice. He wanted to do something about it as quickly as he could.

He ran to Frank's Health Shop and bought all kinds of things for exercising and losing weight, and getting in shape. He had them delivered to his house.

When the exercising gear arrived, Henry put on gym shorts and got to work. He began his fitness plans with the barbells.

Henry pulled and strained with all his might and lifted the barbells. He got them as high as his chest. Then they fell! Henry's feet were crushed!

Henry quit the barbells and sat down on a stool to rest his sore feet. He reached for a wooden pole. He began twisting back and forth with the pole to slim down his waist.

CRASH! The pole smashed Henry's television set!

Henry quit the pole and went to do chin-ups. But the chinning bar came loose! Henry fell to the floor with a bang!

Henry picked himself up and went to work out on the reducing machine. He put the belt around his waist and flipped the button to "on." All at once the machine went wild!

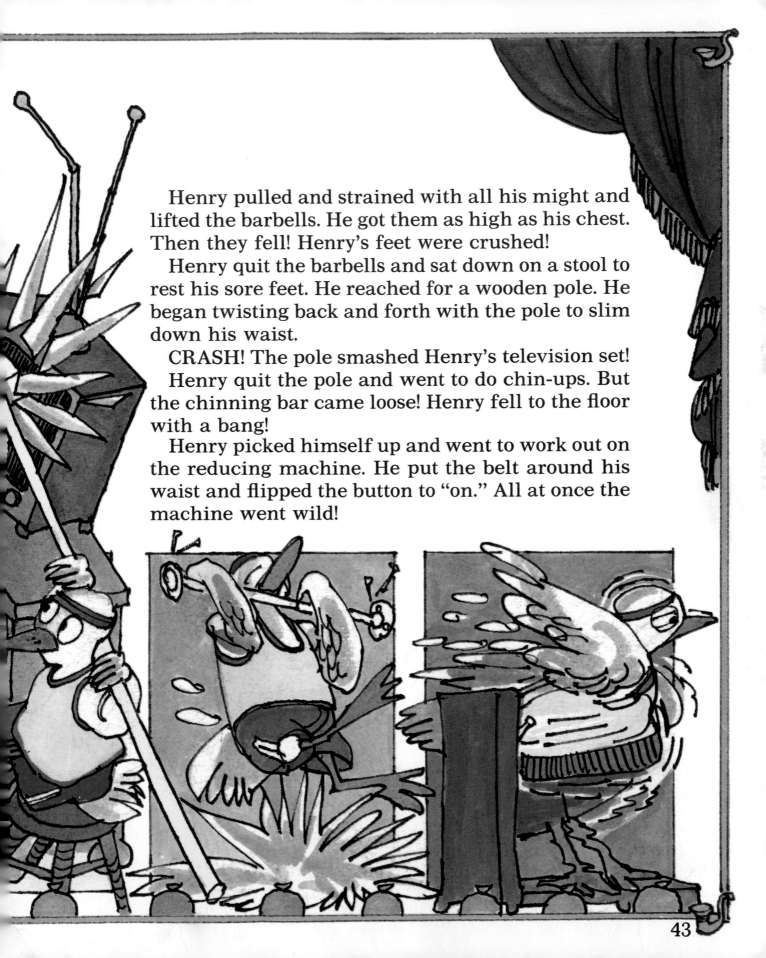

Henry was tossed this way and that. Finally he was tossed out the window. He decided it would be safer to stay outside and go jogging instead.

But Henry had only run a few steps when it started to rain. He got soaking wet and had to go back home.

Inside again Henry climbed on an exercise bike and started pedaling. He was sure that nothing bad could happen on a bike with only one wheel.

But he was wrong. The wheel turned faster and faster as Henry pedaled. Soon the wheel was going so fast he couldn't stop it. He got his feet tangled in the pedals and was thrown from the bike.

By now Henry was sore all over. But he remembered what his scale said when he weighed himself

that morning. He decided jumping rope would be a safe, sure way of exercising. He got the rope and began jumping.

But as he jumped, Henry got tangled in the jumping rope. He fell to the floor, all tied in a knot. Now what was he going to do?

He worked his way across the room to telephone for help. He pushed the dial buttons with his beak and a rescue squad came.

That night, Henry staggered to Clara's house. He was all worn out. And when Clara saw him she was surprised.

"Why, Henry!" she said. "You look out of shape. Forget the movies. What you need is . . .

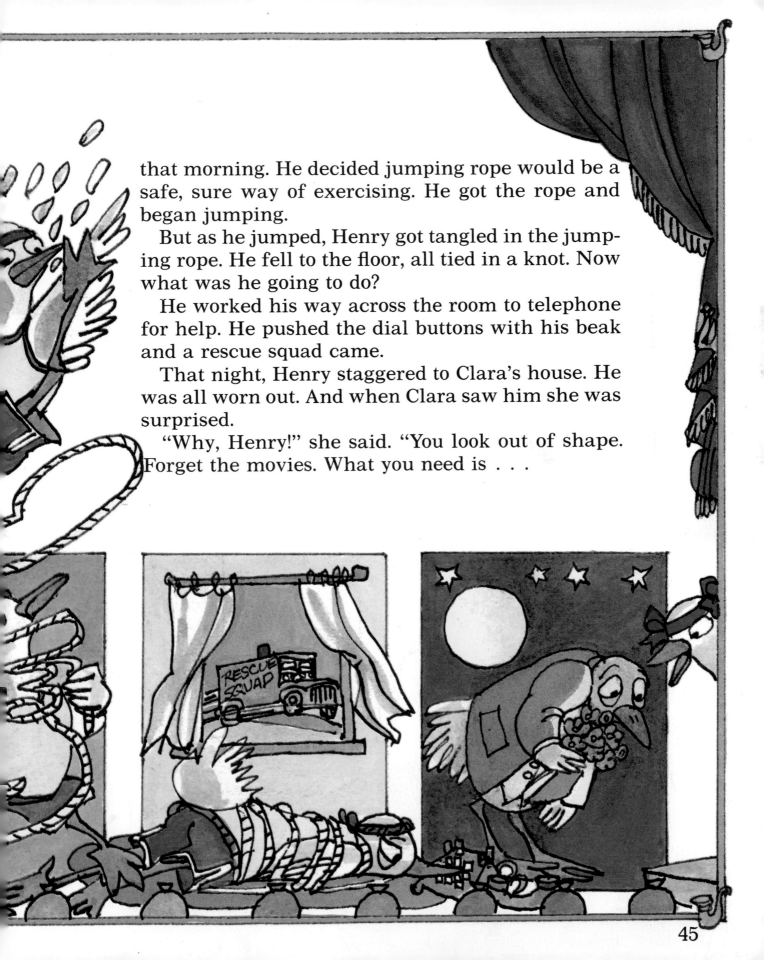

. . . some exercise. Let's go dancing."

YANKEE DOODLE

lively

Yan-kee Doo-dle went to town A-rid-ing on his po-ny, He stuck a fea-ther in his cap And called it mac-a-ro-ni.

Chorus:

Yan-kee Doo-dle, keep it up. Yan-kee Doo-dle dan-dy, Mind the mu-sic and the step And with the girls be han-dy.

2.
Father and I went down to camp
Along with Captain Goodin'
And there we saw the men and boys
As thick as hasty puddin'.
Chorus:

3.
There was Captain Washington
Upon a slapping stallion,
A-giving orders to his men;
I guess there was a million.
Chorus:

4.
There I saw a little keg,
The heads were made of leather.
They knocked upon it with some sticks
To call the folks together.
Chorus:

5.
Then I saw a swamping gun
As big as logs of maple
Upon a mightly little cart,
A load for Father's cattle.
Chorus:

6.
Came the time they shot it off,
It took a horn of powder,
And made a noise like Father's gun,
Only a nation louder.
Chorus:

7.
Scared me so I scampered off
Nor stopped as I remember
Nor turned around till I got home,
Locked safe in Mother's chamber.
Chorus:

No Mouse for Me
~by R.Q.~

Here.
Take back your mouse.
I don't want it.
It could be *dangerous*
for me to keep it.
Because . . .

A cat might come
and chase the mouse
I kept at my house.

Then a dog would come.

The dog would chase the cat.
The cat would chase the mouse.
See what would happen at my house!

Then a dogcatcher would come.
The dogcatcher would chase the dog.
The dog would chase the cat.
The cat would chase the mouse.
See what would happen at my house!

Then the dog's owner would come.
The dog's owner would chase the dogcatcher.
The dogcatcher would chase the dog.
The dog would chase the cat.
The cat would chase the mouse.
See what would happen at my house!

Then the riot squad would come.
The riot squad would chase the dog's owner.
The dog's owner would chase the dogcatcher.
The dogcatcher would chase the dog.
The dog would chase the cat.
The cat would chase the mouse.
See what would happen at my house!

Then the fire department would come.
The fire department would chase the riot squad.
The riot squad would chase the dog's owner.
The dog's owner would chase the dogcatcher.
The dogcatcher would chase the dog.
The dog would chase the cat.
The cat would chase the mouse.
See what would happen at my house!

51

Then the news reporters would come.
The reporters would chase the fire department.
The fire department would chase the riot squad.
The riot squad would chase the dog's owner.
The dog's owner would chase the dogcatcher.
The dogcatcher would chase the dog.
The dog would chase the cat.
The cat would chase the mouse.
See what would happen at my house!

Then the army and navy would come.
The army and navy would chase the reporters.
The reporters would chase the fire department.
The fire department would chase the riot squad.
The riot squad would chase the dog's owner.
The dog's owner would chase the dogcatcher.
The dogcatcher would chase the dog.
The dog would chase the cat.
The cat would chase the mouse.
See what would happen at my house!

MICE
FOR SALE
CHEAP!

Then the air force would come.
The air force would chase the army and navy.
The army and navy would chase the reporters.
The reporters would chase the fire department.
The fire department would chase the riot squad.
The riot squad would chase the dog's owner.
The dog's owner would chase the dogcatcher.
The dogcatcher would chase the dog.
The dog would chase the cat.
The cat would chase the mouse.
See what would happen at my house!

TERRIBLE THINGS WOULD HAPPEN!

And all because of a little mouse.

So give me my money back.

I'd rather have a snake.

Calling Dr. Quack
—by R.Q.—

As Dr. Quack paddled toward his office, he heard a strange noise coming from his waiting room. He listened at the door.

"Glub BLUB," the noise said.

Dr. Quack slowly opened the door. He saw Bert Beaver sitting on the sofa, looking very uncomfortable.

"Glub BLUB," said Bert.

Dr. Quack took the patient into the examining room.

"What is the trouble, Bert?" Dr. Quack asked. "If you can't tell me, show me."

Bert pointed to his throat and Dr. Quack reached for a tongue depressor.

"Let's have a look," said Dr. Quack. "Open wide and say, 'Aaaaaaah.'"

"Aaaaaaah. Glub. Blub. REEBIT!" said Bert.

"Good heavens," said Dr. Quack, as calmly as he could. "You have a frog in your throat!"

Dr. Quack grabbed a pair of forceps.

"Open wide, Bert," he said again. "This will only take a second."

Bert opened wide.

Dr. Quack carefully inserted the forceps, and pulled.

Out popped Herman Frog.

"Whew!" said Herman.

"Thank you, Doctor," said Bert in his own voice.

"You're welcome," said Dr. Quack. "Now, do you mind telling me how it happened? In all my years of practice I have never seen such a case."

"It was an accident," said Bert. "I was resting behind a log. I didn't see Herman sitting on the log and he didn't see me. Suddenly Herman made a leap in the air just as I yawned and he plopped into my throat. I didn't know what to do. So I ran to your office right away."

"You did the correct thing," said Dr. Quack. "But this is my advice to you both. Remember that an ounce of prevention is worth a pound of cure. So from now on, Herman, please look before you leap. And from now on, Bert, please look before you sleep."

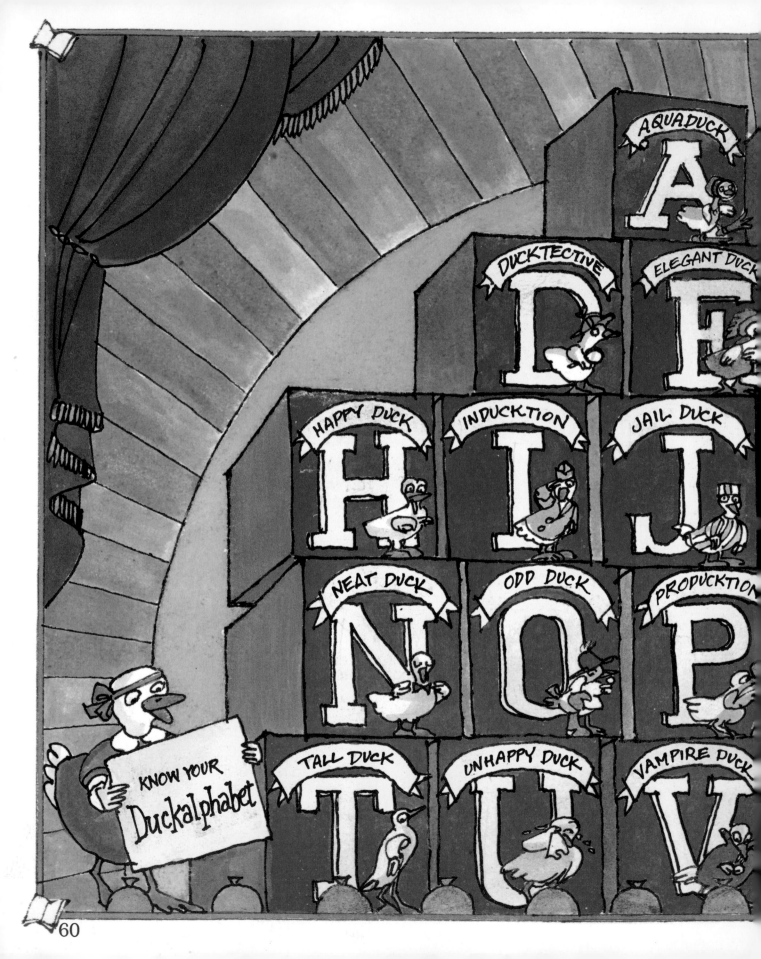

Detective Mole and the Chicken Coop Mystery
~by R.Q.~

Early one morning Detective Mole's phone rang. It was Mrs. Hen calling.

"Help! Help!" she cried. "There's a ghost in our coop. Come at once!"

Detective Mole grabbed his magnifying glass and ran to Chicken Coop Number 5. He was greeted at the door by Mr. Rooster and Mrs. Hen. He asked them to tell him about the ghost.

"For three nights we have heard a spooky voice coming from the attic," said Mr. Rooster. "But when I go up to look, no one is there. It must be a ghost!"

Detective Mole asked what the spooky voice said.

"It is always the same," said Mr. Rooster. "Each night we have heard the terrible words 'DO NOT SEND YOUR CHILDREN TO SCHOOL!'"

"It's horrible," sobbed Mrs. Hen. "The ghost keeps talking about our chicks. I'm sure they are in danger!"

Detective Mole asked if the chicks knew anything about the ghost in the attic. Mrs. Hen said that she hadn't told them about it.

"I thought they would be too frightened!" she said.

"I'm sure the chicks didn't hear the ghost," said Mr. Rooster. "Each time, I looked in their room to see if they were all right. They were sound asleep."

"The little dears are at school now," said Mrs. Hen. "But my husband and I were considering not sending them this morning."

"Hmmmm," said Detective Mole. "May I see the chicks' bedroom?"

Mrs. Hen and Mr. Rooster showed him the way. Detective Mole looked carefully at everything in the room. He even looked out the window. He saw a broken rain pipe next to the window. He studied it with his magnifying glass.

"Hmmmm," he said. "Perhaps I should stay here tonight to hear this ghost for myself."

"But it might upset the chicks if they knew a detective was in the house," said Mrs. Hen.

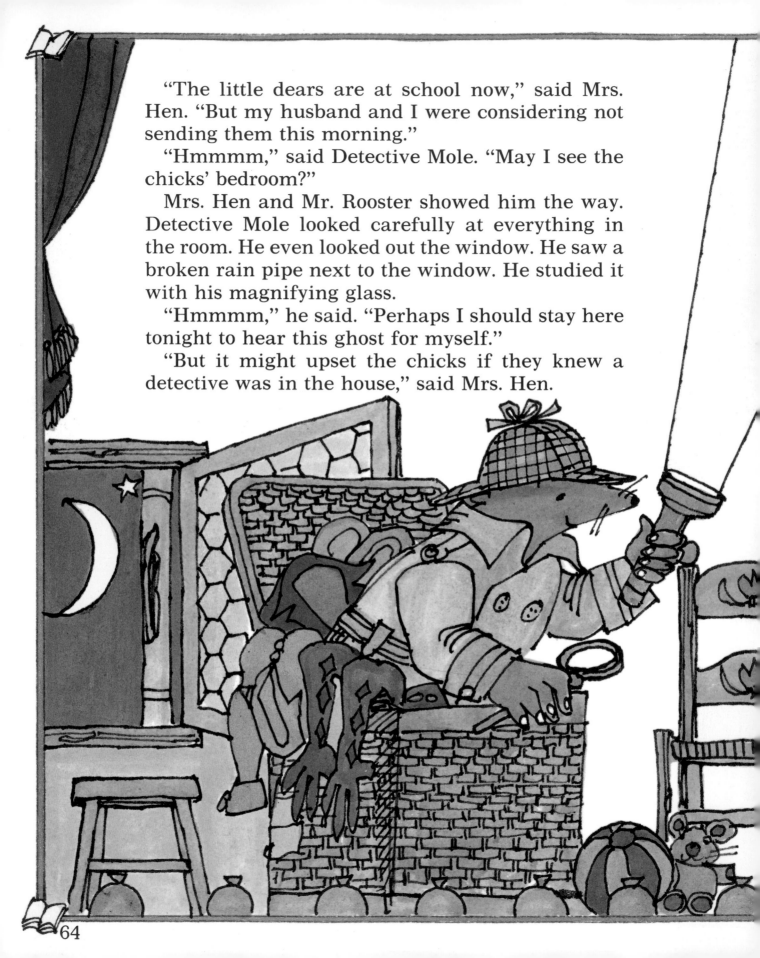

"I could hide somewhere," said Detective Mole.

"What about the clothes hamper?" asked Mrs. Hen.

That night Detective Mole was squashed in the crowded hamper, waiting for the ghost. Just after the clock struck midnight, Detective Mole heard a loud, spooky voice.

"OOOOOOOOOOOOO," said the voice.

"OOOOOOOOOOOOO," it said again.

Then it said, "THIS IS YOUR LAST WARNING! DO NOT SEND YOUR CHILDREN TO SCHOOL!"

Detective Mole climbed carefully out of the clothes hamper. He tiptoed to the door of the chicks' bedroom. He opened the door very quietly.

Suddenly Mrs. Hen and Mr. Rooster, who were frozen with fright in their own room, heard loud cheeping noises. They ran to the chicks' room. They saw Detective Mole holding the chicks by the collars of their nightshirts.

"Aha!" said Detective Mole. "Here is your ghost, caught in the act!"

"Goodness gracious!" said Mrs. Hen. "How can that be?"

Detective Mole told how he had solved the case.

"I saw the rain pipe outside the chicks' bedroom," he said. "There is a hole in it next to their window. I figured that if the chicks spoke through the hole, their voices would echo in the attic."

"Think of that!" said Mr. Rooster.

"You naughty chicks!" said Mrs. Hen. "What a scare you gave us! But thanks to Detective Mole, you have been found out and you will be going to school tomorrow as usual."

And they did.

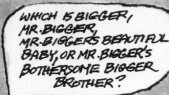

WHICH IS BIGGER, MR. BIGGER, MR. BIGGER'S BEAUTIFUL BABY, OR MR. BIGGER'S BOTHERSOME BIGGER BROTHER?

MR. BIGGER'S BEAUTIFUL BABY IS "A LITTLE BIGGER."

I HOPE I DON'T SEE ANY OF YOU LOOKING AT EACH OTHER'S TEST PAPERS.

I HOPE YOU DON'T EITHER!

MR. SMITH OWNS A VEGETABLE STAND. HE STANDS SIX FEET TALL AND HE IS THIRTY-SIX INCHES AROUND HIS MIDDLE. WHAT DOES HE WEIGH?

FRUITS AND VEGETABLES.

IF YOU HAD TEN PIECES OF CANDY AND SOMEONE ASKED YOU FOR ONE, HOW MANY WOULD YOU HAVE LEFT?

TEN.

THERE ARE ELEVEN COPYCATS SITTING ON A FENCE. ONE JUMPED OFF. HOW MANY WERE LEFT?

NONE.

DID YOU KNOW THAT THE LAW OF GRAVITY KEEPS US FROM FALLING OFF THE EARTH?

SOME LAW. WHAT KEPT US FROM FALLING OFF BEFORE IT WAS PASSED?

STAND WITH YOUR BACK TO THE NORTH AND FACE DUE SOUTH. WHAT WOULD BE ON YOUR LEFT HAND?

FINGERS.

IF YOU ADD 865, 242, AND 22, THEN DIVIDE BY 47, WHAT WOULD YOU GET?

THE WRONG ANSWER.

IN TEN SECONDS, NAME TEN ANIMALS FROM AFRICA.

FIVE LIONS AND FIVE GIRAFFES.

WHAT HAS TWO FEET AND NO LEGS?

TWENTY-FOUR INCHES.

YOU SAY YOU GOT THAT BUMP ON YOUR NOSE FROM SMELLING A BROSE. BUT THERE IS NO "B" IN ROSE.

THERE WAS IN THIS ONE.

YES?

I DON'T WANT TO SCARE YOU, BUT MY DAD SAID IF I DIDN'T GET A GOOD REPORT CARD, SOMEONE'S GOING TO GET A SPANKING.

There Was a Li'l Woman Who Took a Stroll

Monster Jokes and Riddles

WHY DID DRACULA WEAR LONG UNDERWEAR TO THE GALA OPENING OF HIS MOVIE?

BECAUSE THE MOVIE WAS A CHILLER.

WHAT IS PURPLE AND FUZZY AND HAS YELLOW STRIPES?

I DON'T KNOW.

I DON'T KNOW EITHER, BUT IT'S CRAWLING UP YOUR ARM RIGHT NOW.

WHY DID THE BRIDE OF FRANKENSTEIN'S MONSTER SHOOT THE ALARM CLOCK?

SHE FELT LIKE KILLING TIME.

WHY DID DRACULA CHASE THE REFRIGERATOR?

BECAUSE IT WAS RUNNING.

WHAT GOES GREEN, GREEN, GREEN, GREEN?

FRANKENSTEIN'S MONSTER ROLLING DOWN A HILL.

WHAT DID THE BOSS SAY TO HIS SECRETARY WHEN SHE TOLD HIM THAT THE INVISIBLE MAN WAS AT THE DOOR?

"TELL HIM I CAN'T SEE HIM."

HOW DO YOU FEED CHICKEN SOUP TO KING KONG WHEN HE HAS A COLD?

VERY CAREFULLY.

WHY DID THE WEREWOLF TAKE A BATH WHEN THE POLICE CAME?

BECAUSE HE WAS IN HOT WATER.

WHAT HAPPENED WHEN THE PHANTOM OF THE OPERA ATE A LEMON?

HE SANG SOUR NOTES.

WHAT DID THE EXPLORER SAY WHEN HE WAS LOST IN THE EGYPTIAN TOMB?

"I WANT MY MUMMY!"

HOW DOES FRANKENSTEIN'S MONSTER MAKE A STRAWBERRY SHAKE?

HE TAKES IT TO A HORROR MOVIE.

WHY DO MONSTERS GO TO PARADES?

BECAUSE THEY LIKE DEMON-STRATIONS.

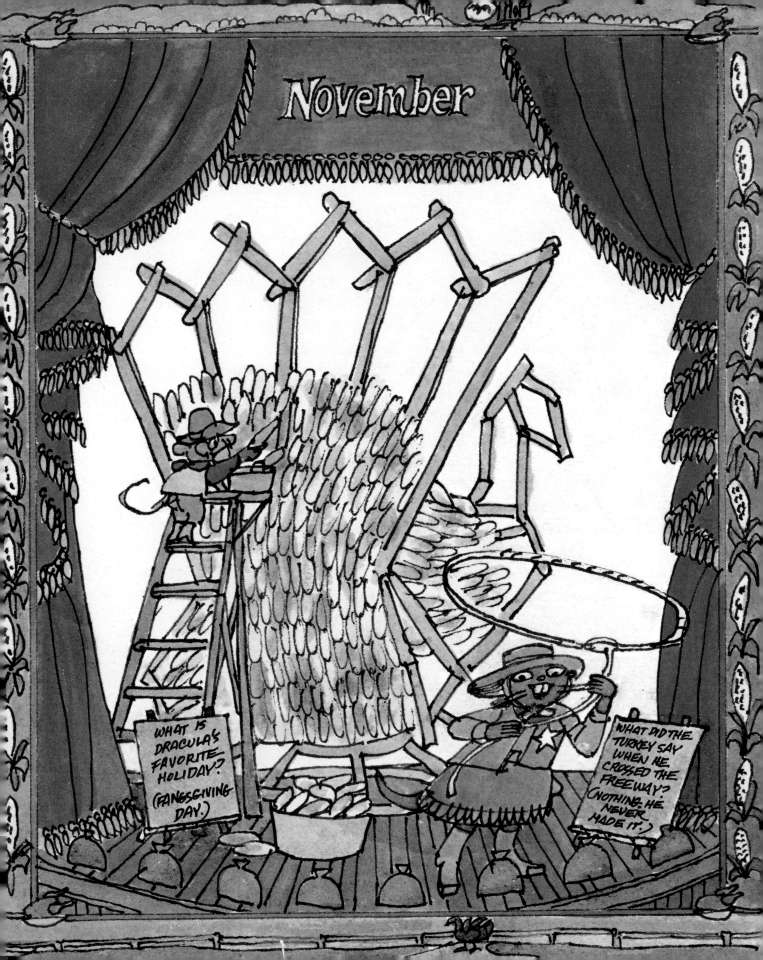

Sheriff Sally Gopher and the Thanksgiving Caper

~by R.Q.~

Virgil Vulture stormed into Sheriff Sally Gopher's office.

"I protest!" he cried. "The statue of Terence Turkey in the square is a fake! Halt the work!"

Virgil Vulture's objections were so loud that the sheriff's dozing deputies—Summers and Winters Jack Rabbit, Rosa Roadrunner, and Gracie Gecko—fell out of their chairs.

"What do you mean, Virgil?" said Sheriff Sally, looking out the window that faced the town square. "It looks like ol' Terence Turkey to me, and he's always been the model for Pebble Junction's Thanksgiving corn feast. After all, it was his ancestor Miles Turkey who graced the table at the first Thanksgiving and who became a national symbol. So the statue *should* look like Terence."

"That's just it!" cried Virgil. "Why does Terence get all the honors? My ancestor Jonathan Vulture was also at the Pilgrims' first Thanksgiving."

"He was?" cried Sheriff Sally Gopher and her astonished deputies.

"Of course he was," snapped Virgil. "Everyone knows what valuable scavengers we vultures are. Who do you think cleaned up the mess after the feast?"

"Ugh, disgusting," said the Jack Rabbit twins.

"Quiet, deputies," said Sheriff Sally. "Virgil has a right to be heard. Let's see the mayor about this, Virgil," she went on, following the vulture outside. "I'd like to know what *he* says."

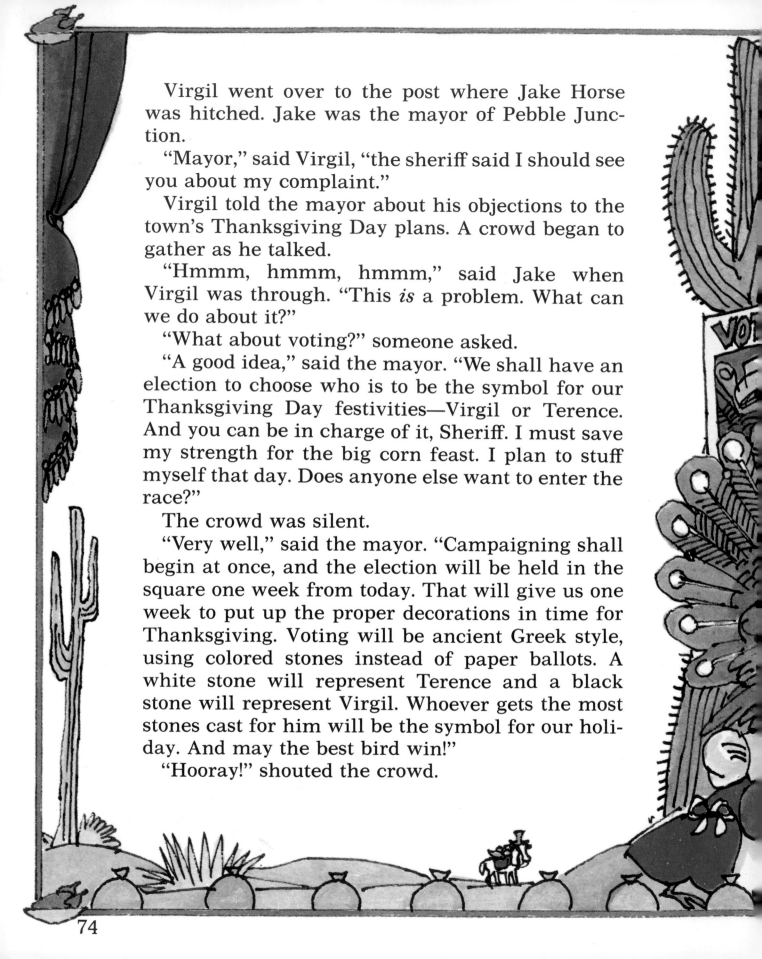

Virgil went over to the post where Jake Horse was hitched. Jake was the mayor of Pebble Junction.

"Mayor," said Virgil, "the sheriff said I should see you about my complaint."

Virgil told the mayor about his objections to the town's Thanksgiving Day plans. A crowd began to gather as he talked.

"Hmmm, hmmm, hmmm," said Jake when Virgil was through. "This *is* a problem. What can we do about it?"

"What about voting?" someone asked.

"A good idea," said the mayor. "We shall have an election to choose who is to be the symbol for our Thanksgiving Day festivities—Virgil or Terence. And you can be in charge of it, Sheriff. I must save my strength for the big corn feast. I plan to stuff myself that day. Does anyone else want to enter the race?"

The crowd was silent.

"Very well," said the mayor. "Campaigning shall begin at once, and the election will be held in the square one week from today. That will give us one week to put up the proper decorations in time for Thanksgiving. Voting will be ancient Greek style, using colored stones instead of paper ballots. A white stone will represent Terence and a black stone will represent Virgil. Whoever gets the most stones cast for him will be the symbol for our holiday. And may the best bird win!"

"Hooray!" shouted the crowd.

With that, Jake Horse called the meeting to an end—and everyone ran to get ready for the election. The corn statue of Terence was taken down, and election posters and banners were placed around the town.

Sheriff Sally Gopher maintained order during the campaign. She assigned posts to each of her deputies, who were to report anything that might keep the election from being a fair and honest one.

"I promise to make this coming Thanksgiving Day one that you will never forget," cried Virgil Vulture in his campaign speech. "Vote for me."

A few paces away Terence Turkey proclaimed, "I promise to carry on as the true symbol of Thanksgiving Day. Vote for me!"

Campaign week passed quickly, and soon Election Day arrived. The voting booth was set up in the square. One at a time, the voters entered the booth and dropped their secret stones into the ballot box.

That afternoon Summers Jack Rabbit burst into Sheriff Sally's office and said, "The first box of stones was just counted, Sheriff. Terence is in the lead. It looks like the turkey symbol may stay."

Just then Virgil Vulture passed by the open door and overheard the deputy's report. "Don't be so sure," he said from the doorway. "Don't be so sure." Turning abruptly, he stomped off again.

"Let's keep an eye on him, Summers," said Sheriff Sally.

The sheriff and her deputy followed Virgil to the square. The vulture was the last to vote. He entered the booth with a little paper sack, like the ones other voters had carried to hide their stones.

After Virgil had voted the judges emptied the ballot box for the second and last time. To their surprise all the stones were black. They counted them and wrote the final results on the tally board. Virgil had won!

The crowd went wild. Some citizens were happy, some were sad, and some shouted, "Recount! Recount!" Things were getting out of hand, so Sheriff Sally stepped forward.

"Listen, everyone!" she cried. "We are losing valuable time from our Thanksgiving preparations. Virgil has won. Arguing about it might delay our feast day. It's just a symbol that has been changed —not our whole wonderful holiday. Can't we bring this election to a close?"

There were nods and cheers, and soon everyone agreed that Sally was right and that Virgil was the rightful winner. Then the townspeople set to work redoing their Thanksgiving decorations. The statue in the square was made to look like Virgil, and so were all the favors. As the days went by, though, it became clear that something was wrong.

"What gloom seems to have settled over this town!" Gracie Gecko blurted out one afternoon.

"The decorations don't help," said Summers Jack Rabbit. "It seems strange to have a vulture for our Thanksgiving symbol."

"That's for sure," agreed Winters Jack Rabbit.

"Quiet, deputies," said Sheriff Sally. "You'll just upset folks with your complaints."

It was too late. Mother Quail had heard them talking.

"Your deputies are right, Sheriff," she said. "There *is* gloom cast over what should be a happy time for everyone. Can't Virgil be stopped? I hear that he is even changing the menu from Indian corn recipes to things only *he* likes."

Just then a small black object whizzed past Sheriff Sally's foot and landed in a puddle. It was a quail chick's marble, and Sheriff Sally went to rescue it. But when she picked it out of the water it was no longer black. It was white!

"That's strange, chicks," said Sheriff Sally. "Where did you get this marble? It appears to have been painted."

"It's one of the stones from the election," explained a chick. "The judges gave them to us so we could play marbles. See? They are all like that one."

"You don't say," said Sheriff Sally. "Let me borrow a few of them. I'll return them to you in a jiffy."

Sheriff Sally took her deputies aside.

"Someone colored these stones so that the election would come out in Virgil's favor," she said. "But who?"

"What about Virgil himself?" said Summers Jack Rabbit. "He was the last to vote. He could have poured a bottle of quick-drying ink into the ballot box."

"Of course!" cried Sheriff Sally. "Let's go talk to him."

They all ran to Virgil's house. In the trash can in his yard they found the paper sack he had carried into the voting booth. Inside the bag was an empty bottle of black ink!

"Nice try, Virgil," said Sheriff Sally, holding up the evidence. "But cheaters never win. It's a good thing for you that it wasn't a regular election, or I would have to haul you in and lock you up. I have a good mind to, anyway, and throw away the key."

"Please don't do that to me," Virgil begged. "I made a mistake. I don't really want to be the feast symbol. We vultures are loners. We hate huge gatherings. Give the job to Terence. He really should have won."

"I'm glad you feel that way, Virgil," said Sheriff Sally.

With only two days left till Thanksgiving, the townspeople worked at fever pitch to set everything right again.

By the time the big day rolled around, the election was forgotten and Virgil was forgiven. He was the only one to stay home, waiting, as he always did, for his fun to begin at cleanup time.

So, in the end, Pebble Junction's holiday was a perfect success. It was so perfect that everyone vowed to keep to tradition at future Thanksgivings. And they stuck to their word.

The Nutcrackers and the Sugar-Tongs

—by EDWARD LEAR—

The Nutcrackers sate by a plate on the table,
  The Sugar-tongs sate by a plate at his side;
And the Nutcrackers said, "Don't you wish we were able
  Along the blue hills and green meadows to ride?
Must we drag on this stupid existence for ever,
  So idle and weary, so full of remorse, —
While every one else takes his pleasure, and never
  Seems happy unless he is riding a horse?

Don't you think we could ride without being instructed?
  Without any saddle, or bridle, or spur?
Our legs are so long, and so aptly constructed,
  I'm sure that an accident could not occur.
Let us all of a sudden hop down from the table,
  And hustle downstairs, and each jump on a horse!
Shall we try? Shall we go? Do you think we are able?"
  The Sugar-tongs answered distinctly, "Of course!"

So down the long staircase they hopped in a minute,
  The Sugar-tongs snapped, and the Crackers said "crack!"
The stable was open, the horses were in it;
  Each took out a pony, and jumped on his back.
The Cat in a fright scrambled out of the doorway,
  The Mice tumbled out of a bundle of hay,
The brown and white Rats, and the black ones from Norway,
Screamed out, "They are taking the horses away!"

The whole of the household was filled with amazement,
  The Cups and the Saucers danced madly about,
The Plates and the Dishes looked out of the casement,
  The Saltcellar stood on his head with a shout,
The Spoons with a clatter looked out of the lattice,
  The Mustard-pot climbed up the Gooseberry Pies,
The Soup-ladle peeped through a heap of Veal Patties,
  And squeaked with a ladle-like scream of surprise.

The Frying-pan said, "It's an awful delusion!"
  The Tea-kettle hissed and grew black in the face;
And they all rushed downstairs in the wildest confusion,
  To see the great Nutcracker–Sugar-tong race.
And out of the stable, with screamings and laughter
  (Their ponies were cream-coloured, speckled with brown,)
The Nutcrackers first, and the Sugar-tongs after,
  Rode all around the yard, and then all round the town.

They rode through the street, and they rode by the station,
  They galloped away to the beautiful shore;
In silence they rode, and made no observation,
  Save this: "We will never go back any more!"
And still you might hear, till they rode out of hearing,
  The Sugar-tongs snap, and the Crackers say "crack!"
Till far in the distance their forms disappearing,
  They faded away. —And they never came back!

The Boy Who Waited for Santa Claus

—by R.Q.—

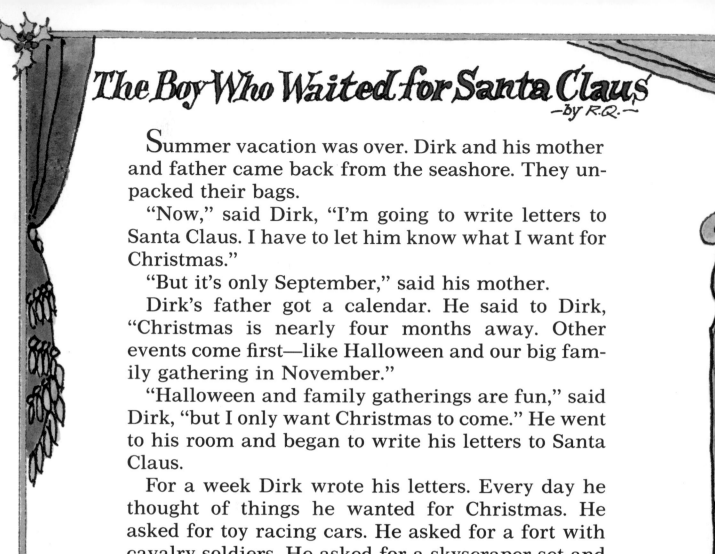

Summer vacation was over. Dirk and his mother and father came back from the seashore. They unpacked their bags.

"Now," said Dirk, "I'm going to write letters to Santa Claus. I have to let him know what I want for Christmas."

"But it's only September," said his mother.

Dirk's father got a calendar. He said to Dirk, "Christmas is nearly four months away. Other events come first—like Halloween and our big family gathering in November."

"Halloween and family gatherings are fun," said Dirk, "but I only want Christmas to come." He went to his room and began to write his letters to Santa Claus.

For a week Dirk wrote his letters. Every day he thought of things he wanted for Christmas. He asked for toy racing cars. He asked for a fort with cavalry soldiers. He asked for a skyscraper set and a drawbridge that went up and down. Then he put stamps on his letters and sent them off. Now all he had to do was wait for Santa Claus.

The following Saturday Dirk's mother suggested a family picnic.

"I can't go with you," said Dirk. "Why not?" asked his father.

"I'm waiting for Santa Claus," said Dirk. "What if he comes while we are out? I'd better stay at home."

And so it was every day. Dirk wouldn't go out for any reason. He only wanted to stay at home and wait for Santa Claus.

Then school started. Dirk *had* to go out. But always, after school, he would head straight home to wait for Santa.

Halloween came. His parents asked Dirk which costume he would like to wear.

"None," he said. "I'm waiting for Santa Claus."

After Halloween several of his friends had birthdays. Dirk was invited to parties, but he didn't want to go. He asked, "How many days to Christmas?"

Dirk got an invitation to attend his best friend Jeremy's birthday party.

"This is one party you can't turn down, Dirk," said his mother. "Jeremy will be hurt if you're not there."

Dirk *did* go to Jeremy's party. But he didn't enjoy himself very much. He was in a hurry for the party to be over so he could be back at home, waiting for Santa Claus.

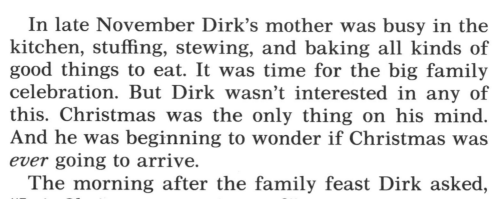

In late November Dirk's mother was busy in the kitchen, stuffing, stewing, and baking all kinds of good things to eat. It was time for the big family celebration. But Dirk wasn't interested in any of this. Christmas was the only thing on his mind. And he was beginning to wonder if Christmas was *ever* going to arrive.

The morning after the family feast Dirk asked, "Is it Christmas morning yet?"

Dirk's father answered jokingly, "No, there are some more holidays coming up like Peanut Day when we all dress up like nuts."

It was the wrong thing to say. Dirk burst into tears.

"I don't want any more holidays," Dirk sobbed. "I want Christmas."

His father ran over and said he was sorry for teasing him and gave him a big hug. Dirk stopped crying. He went back to waiting.

Suddenly Christmas shows began appearing on television. Dirk knew Christmas was coming soon.

Every night he watched the shows. But that made waiting even harder. So Dirk stopped watching television. He went to bed earlier and earlier. He didn't even stay up to help his mother bake delicious things for Christmas. He was too worn out from waiting.

At last Christmas morning arrived. There under the Christmas tree were all the presents that Dirk had asked Santa to bring him. Everything was just as he hoped it would be. But wait! Where was the fort he wanted? Had Santa Claus forgotten to bring it? Dirk was worried.

Then Dirk saw a big box hidden away under a branch of the Christmas tree. He pulled it out and tore off the ribbon. He opened the box. Inside was the fort! And the cavalry soldiers too!

"Oh, thank you, Santa Claus!" cried Dirk. "I knew you wouldn't forget!"

When the presents were all opened, Dirk's mother and father looked at one another happily. Santa Claus had come at last. Now they could all go out as a family again.

"We could all go see the outdoor Christmas displays before they are taken down," said Dirk's mother.

"Perhaps I can still get tickets for all of us to go together to see a Christmas play," said Dirk's father.

Dirk listened.

"I can't go with you," he said.

His mother and father turned and looked at him. "Why not?" they asked together.

"Because I have to stay home and wait for something," said Dirk.

"FOR WHAT?" cried his mother and father.

"My birthday," said Dirk. "It's on April 29, you know."

About the Captain of This Showboat

Since 1962, Robert Quackenbush has been delighting young readers with his humor. He has written and illustrated over one hundred and fifty books. His story characters have become known all over the world. Whenever he speaks before audiences of children—which is frequent and has included author tours from Alaska to South America—he is introduced as the father of Henry the Duck, Detective Mole, Miss Mallard, Pete Pack Rat, Sheriff Sally Gopher, and many more. He is the three-time winner of the American Flag Institute Award for outstanding contributions to children's literature and winner of an Edgar Allan Poe special award for best juvenile mystery. He resides in New York City with his wife and young son Piet, who has been the inspiration for many of his stories.

This treasury of humor includes some of Mr. Quackenbush's beloved stories and jokes, some of his favorite rhymes, poems, songs, and limericks by authors such as Edward Lear and Lewis Carroll, and some never-before-published original Quackenbush stories and humor that feature his well-known book characters. Look for some new characters, too! Everything has been freshly illustrated by Mr. Quackenbush with pen and ink and watercolor on Arches paper in the manner of a showboat presentation. Enjoy the show!